BLENDER COOKBOOK

paul mayer

TAYLOR TRADE PUBLISHING

Blender Cookbook, a nitty gritty® Cookbook

Produced by CulinartMedia, Inc.
Design: Harrah Lord
Layout: Patty Holden
Editor: Daniella Malfitano
Photography: Eising Food Photography (all rights reserved)
www.culinartmedia.com

Distributed by National Book Network
1-800-462-6420

ISBN 978-1-58979-882-3
Library of Congress Cataloguing-in-Publication Data on file

Printed in China

CONTENTS

THE BASICS

A blender can help you to easily prepare elegant dishes, which normally take considerable time and labor, by eliminating some of the lengthy mixing procedures. For example, when using the blender to mix a cake, the butter, eggs, sugar, milk, and flavorings are blended together a few seconds and then added to the flour. Cream sauces are free of lumps and egg-based sauces such as hollandaise, bearnaise and mayonnaise are easily prepared without the usual problem of separating.

This book will not tell you how to make frozen daquiris, prepare frozen orange juice or any of the other everyday blender miracles you have already read about in the booklet which came with your blender. In the Blender Cookbook, I will tell you how to prepare gourmet and traditional recipes as prepared at the Paul Mayer Cooking School in San Francisco. The emphasis will be on ease of preparation with the help of a blender. I will instruct you on how to produce soups, sauces, pâtés, hors d'oeuvres, vegetables and salad dressings of the highest quality.

Before you begin, I would like to point out a few basic lessons from my cooking school to make your life in the kitchen more pleasant and successful.

POINTS TO REMEMBER

• Before starting any recipe, sit down and read it carefully. Be sure you have all of the ingredients and enough time to prepare the dish.

• Line up ingredients and utensils in one place before starting.

• Prepare equipment in advance. Be sure that all pans are buttered and floured, and that butter and chocolate are melted, if required.

• Adjust racks and preheat oven to the proper temperature.

• Always remember that common sense is the most important ingredient in any recipe. Don't follow along on blind faith. Your oven may be 50 degrees higher or lower than the one in the test kitchen, or your altitude may differ, or other variables may exist. Be observant and test for doneness to your own satisfaction.

• And, last but not least, enjoy yourself! Cooking can be one of life's most creative and rewarding experiences.

Now, with these instructions well in mind, get out your blender and begin.

Hors d'oeuvres are more than just dainty tidbits to be hand-held at cocktail parties. They are also the small but elegant first course served at the table.

In France, even a family lunch or dinner always begins with an hors d'oeuvre. Attractively arranged and decorated with bright green chopped parsley, this first course often includes leftovers from a previous meal. It is a thrifty and enjoyable method of using up yesterday's green beans, extra hard-cooked eggs, a few shrimp or the end of a roast. A thrifty French housewife also knows that a beginning course also has the advantage of making an expensive meat course go farther.

I have chosen a variety of recipes to present to you here. Many of them were collected on my trips to Europe and are my favorites. Some can be eaten out of hand, while others are more elegant and must be served on a plate with a fork, preferably at the table. You'll enjoy using your blender to make them.

HORS D'OEUVRES

MARINATED PRAWNS

1 lb. medium-sized shrimp
1⅓ cups olive oil
⅔ cup tarragon vinegar
Salt
Black pepper
Paprika
1 large onion, cut in pieces

1 clove garlic
3 Tbsp. Dijon mustard
1 Tbsp. German-style mustard
2 tsp. horseradish
1 tsp. powdered thyme
Sesame seeds for garnish

Cover shrimp with salted water. Bring just to boil. Drain. Rinse under cold water to stop further cooking. Remove the shrimp shells and clean the shrimp by making a shallow cut on the spine and pull out the vein. Place remaining ingredients in blender container. Blend on low speed 15 to 30 seconds or until onion is chopped. Pour the dressing over shrimp and let marinate in refrigerator overnight or until well chilled. Pour into colander and drain off as much dressing as possible. Serve in shallow bowl and garnish the top with sesame seeds.

STEAK À LA TARTARE

½ lb. lean round or sirloin steak
Salt
3 egg yolks
1 Tbsp. Dijon mustard
¼ cup olive oil

Freshly ground black pepper
15 drops Worcestershire sauce
½ tsp. ketchup
1 Tbsp. each parsley, capers, and onion
Finely chopped chives

Have butcher grind meat finely, but only once. Gently shape the ground meat into a large flat patty. Salt surface liberally. Place egg yolks, mustard, olive oil, and a generous grinding of pepper in blender container. Run blender on highest speed 15 to 30 seconds or until mixture thickens and resembles mayonnaise. Remove lid. Add Worcestershire sauce, ketchup, parsley, chives, capers, and onion; cover and blend for 10 seconds. Place salted meat in mixing bowl. Pour over blended mixture. Mix with hands gently but well and shape neatly on serving dish. Sprinkle with chives and serve raw with crackers or hot toast.

SARDINE-STUFFED LEMONS

6 lemons
2 cans (3¾ oz. each) sardines
5 oz. (10 Tbsp.) butter

1 Tbsp. Dijon mustard
Paprika, pepper
½ tsp. crushed thyme

Cut tops from lemons. Scoop out the pulp using a grapefruit knife. Place sardines, butter, and mustard in blender container. Cover. Blend on high speed until mixture is well puréed. Season with paprika, pepper, a little lemon juice and pulp, and thyme. Blend on high speed 10 to 15 seconds. Fill lemon shells with mixture using a pastry tube with large star tip if available. Chill mixture thoroughly. Garnish each star with a caper. Serve with crackers or hot buttered toast.

CANAPÉ DE FROMAGE

6 slices bacon
2 Tbsp. butter
2 Tbsp. flour
Garlic salt, cayenne
½ cup cream

1 cup Gruyère cheese chunks
½ small onion
1 beaten egg
Paprika, Dijon mustard, Worcestershire sauce
8 slices bread

Cook bacon until very crisp. Drain well. Place bacon, butter, flour, garlic salt, cayenne, cream, Gruyère, and onion in blender container. Cover. Blend on high speed until cheese is grated, about 30 seconds. Pour into saucepan. Stir over moderate heat until sauce thickens and boils and cheese is melted. Do not be alarmed if it is over-buttery at this point. Add beaten egg. Season with paprika, mustard, and a little Worcestershire sauce. Spread on flat plate. Cover with plastic wrap. Chill. Trim crusts from bread. Toast on one side only. Spread untoasted side with softened butter and toast. Cool. Spread generously with chilled cheese mixture. Sprinkle with paprika. Cut into strips or squares. Run under the broiler until crusty and browned. Serve hot!

CHICKEN LIVER PÂTÉ

1 lb. fresh chicken livers
½ cup (¼ lb.) butter
1 medium onion, finely chopped

Salt, pepper, Tabasco
1 tsp. ground coriander
½ cup brandy

Place livers in a small saucepan. Barely cover with cold water. Bring slowly to boil. Reduce heat. Simmer very gently 10 minutes. Drain livers thoroughly. Place in blender container. Melt butter in small skillet. Add onion. Cook slowly without browning until soft. Put in blender container. Add salt, pepper, a drop or two of Tabasco, coriander, and brandy. Cover. Blend on highest speed 30 seconds to 1 minute or until blended and smooth. Pour into crock or a mold which has been lined with aspic. If you do use an aspic lined mold, be sure the pâté is well-chilled before adding, lest you melt the aspic. Chill. Press plastic wrap firmly against surface of pâté to prevent it from drying.

CROQUE-MONSIEUR SAUCE

2 Tbsp. butter
2 Tbsp. flour
1 cup (½ pint) whipping cream
Salt, dry mustard
2 egg yolks

Place butter, flour, cream, salt, and mustard in blender container. Cover. Blend on medium speed until well mixed. Pour into saucepan. Stir over moderate heat until mixture boils. Beat egg yolks. Add a little of the hot sauce, beating rapidly. Return to saucepan. Stir briskly until sauce thickens. Pour into serving dish. Pass sauce with sandwiches.

CROQUE-MONSIEUR
MAKES 36 TRIANGLES

½ lb. Gruyère cheese
Whipping cream
18 slices of bread
9 thin ham slices
3 eggs
3 Tbsp. water

Cut cheese into small pieces. Place in blender container. Cover. Blend on medium speed until cheese is grated. Remove cover. Slowly pour in enough cream to make a paste which will spread easily but not run. Lay bread slices in such a fashion as to have every other one opposing its neighbors so when closed the slices will match. Spread each slice with a thin layer of cheese mixture. On 9 slices place a slice of ham. Close sandwiches. Trim off crusts. Cut each into 4 triangular pieces by slicing from corner to corner. Lightly grease a heavy skillet. Heat. Combine eggs and water. Dip each sandwich triangle. Fry on each side until nicely browned. Let rest a minute or two before serving to allow cheese to set slightly. Arrange sandwich triangles on platter. Garnish with parsley. If desired, serve with the Croque-Monsieur Sauce, recipe on left.

I love soups and I enjoy preparing them the easy blender way.

Soups make perfect meal starters. A cup of soup whets the appetite for the meal to follow like nothing else can. When soup is served at the beginning of a meal, the salad is usually served following the entrée where it serves to clear the palate and prepare it for what comes next. This is typical of French meals and preferred by many Americans.

Bowls of steaming hot soup are extremely inviting on a chilly day or as a late night supper. Equally enjoyable are iced soups on a warm summer day. No matter what the season, a wholesome, delicious meal can be built around a hearty soup, crusty bread and a salad. Fruit and cheese make a fine finish.

Once you've seen how easily soups can be made with the help of a blender, you'll start brightening up your meals with these favorites.

SOUPS

POTAGE CRÈME NIVERNAISE
SERVES 4 TO 6

7 to 8 carrots
¼ cup butter
1 tsp. sugar
½ tsp. salt
¼ cup water

¼ cup flour
Salt, cayenne pepper
2½ cups milk
½ cup whipping cream
Parsley or mint

Peel and slice carrots. Melt 2 tablespoons butter in saucepan. Add carrots, sugar, salt and water. Cover. Cook slowly 20 minutes. Add remaining butter to pan. Stir until melted. Remove from heat. Add flour, salt, and cayenne to taste. Stir in milk. Cook over medium heat, stirring constantly, until soup boils. Reduce heat. Cook slowly until thick, at least 25 minutes. Put thickened mixture into blender container. Cover. Blend on highest speed 15 to 30 seconds, or until velvety smooth. Return to saucepan. Add cream and reheat. Serve steaming hot. Garnish with parsley or finely chopped mint.

ICED CREAM OF CUCUMBER SOUP

SERVES 4 TO 6

3 large cucumbers
2 Tbsp. melted butter
2 whole shallots
6 Tbsp. flour
3 cups chicken broth
1 cup milk, scalded

2 to 3 sprigs mint
½ cup whipping cream
Salt, white pepper
Sour cream
Cucumber slices
Chopped mint

Peel, seed, and coarsely chop cucumbers. Place in blender container with butter and shallots. Blend on medium speed 15 to 30 seconds. Pour into saucepan. Cook slowly 20 minutes. Return mixture to blender container. Add flour, chicken broth, milk, and mint sprigs. Cover. Blend until ingredients are thoroughly blended. Return to saucepan. Stir over moderate heat until soup boils. Add cream. Season to taste with salt and pepper. Chill thoroughly. Serve garnished with sour cream, unpeeled cucumber slices and chopped mint.

TOMATO & DILL SOUP
SERVES 4 TO 6

This soup is equally good served hot or cold.

2 Tbsp. vegetable oil
1 Tbsp. butter
1 onion, finely sliced
1 clove garlic
Salt, black pepper
3 large tomatoes, sliced
1 can (6 oz.) tomato paste

6 Tbsp. flour
2 cups water
¾ cup cream, whipped
1 Tbsp. finely minced fresh dill
    or 1 Tbsp. dried dill weed
Fresh dill sprigs for garnish

Heat oil and butter in saucepan. Add onion, garlic, salt, and pepper. Cook slowly until onion is soft for about 5 to 6 minutes. Increase the heat and add the tomato slices. Cook briskly for 3 minutes and then remove from heat. Add tomato paste and flour and stir in water. Return to medium heat. Stir constantly until mixture comes to a full boil. Next, pass the mixture through a fine strainer and pour into blender container. Cover tightly and bend on high speed for 15 to 30 seconds. Return to pan, add cream and dill and reheat. Serve hot or well chilled. Garnish the top with fresh dill sprigs.

CRÈME HAMILTON

SERVES 4 TO 6

½ lb. mushrooms
3 Tbsp. butter
2 tsp. potato starch
¼ cup milk

½ cup cream, whipped
Whipped cream for garnish
Finely chopped chives*

Place mushrooms in blender container. Cover. Blend on low speed 30 seconds, or until mushrooms are coarsely chopped. Place in saucepan. Allow to stew gently over low heat until mushrooms are very soft. Remove from heat, add 2 tablespoons butter. Stir until melted. Return to blender. Add remaining butter and potato starch (sometimes called potato flour). Blend on highest speed 15 to 30 seconds, or until completely smooth. Pour back into saucepan. Stir over moderate heat until soup boils. It will be very thick. Add milk. Gently fold in whipped cream. This is a rich soup. Serve in demitasse cups, topped with a tiny bit of whipped cream and chives.

*I find the Armanino freeze dried chives completely acceptable for every dish requiring chives in any form.

POTATO & WATERCRESS SOUP

SERVES 4 TO 6

4 medium potatoes*
1 medium onion
2 Tbsp. butter
1 cup water

Salt, white pepper, to taste
1 bunch watercress
1 cup (½ pt.) whipping cream
Fresh dill for garnish

Peel and thinly slice potatoes and onion. Melt butter in deep saucepan and then add the vegetables. Toss to coat with butter. Add water, salt, and pepper and cover pan. Cook slowly until potatoes are thoroughly soft. Coarsely chop watercress. Add to potato mixture. Stir until soup boils and then remove it from heat. Pour into blender container and cover tightly. Blend on highest speed for 15 to 30 seconds or until mixture is smooth. Return to saucepan and add cream to soup. Bring temperature up just to warm. Taste and adjust for seasoning and serve steaming. Garnish the top with fresh dill.

*preferably not Idahos

CREAM OF ONION SOUP

SERVES 4 TO 6

8 onions	2 cups hot milk
¼ cup butter	1–2 cups (½–1 pt.) whipping cream
6 Tbsp. flour	Gruyère cheese, grated
Salt, cayenne pepper, to taste	Nutmeg

Slice onions. Place in pan. Barely cover with boiling water. Cook slowly until onions are tender. Place in blender container. Cover. Blend 15 to 30 seconds. Add butter, flour, salt, cayenne, and milk. Cover. Blend on highest speed 15 to 30 seconds. Pour into saucepan. Stir over medium heat until mixture boils. Remove from heat. Thin to desired consistency with cream. Correct seasoning. Reheat. Allow to simmer gently 3 minutes. Pour into flame-proof tureen. Sprinkle surface with grated Gruyère cheese and a dash of nutmeg. Run under hot broiler until cheese glazes and begins to crust. Serve at once.

POTAGE SIMON

SERVES 4 TO 6

2 bunches carrots
6 Tbsp. butter
Salt, cayenne pepper
1 Tbsp. sugar
1½ cups water

2 bunches spinach
½ cup flour
1 cup chicken broth
3 cups milk

Peel and slice carrots. Melt butter in deep saucepan. Add carrots, salt, cayenne, and sugar. Stir to coat carrots. Add water. Cover. Cook slowly for 5 minutes. Add well-washed spinach. Cook, covered, until carrots are soft. Remove from heat. Pour contents into blender container. Add flour, broth, and milk. Cover. Blend at highest speed 15 to 30 seconds. Return soup to saucepan. Cook, stirring constantly until it boils. If too thick, thin with additional milk. Correct seasoning. Serve hot.

For a Polynesian-type soup, add 1 to 2 tablespoons Japanese oyster sauce. Serve in oven-proof dishes. Top with whipped cream. Run under the broiler until cream has melted and turned brown. Serve sizzling.

POTAGE PAUL

SERVES 4 TO 6

1 Tbsp. butter
2 Tbsp. vegetable oil
1 onion, finely chopped
1 clove garlic
2 pkg. (10 oz. ea.) frozen peas
Salt, pepper

1 scant Tbsp. curry powder
2½ Tbsp. flour
2 cups chicken broth
½–1 cup (½ pt.) whipping cream
⅔ cup chicken, finely minced

Heat butter and oil together. Add onion and garlic. Cook slowly, 3 minutes. Add peas, salt, pepper, and curry. Continue cooking slowly until peas are soft. Remove from heat. Blend in flour. Stir in broth. Return to heat. Stir until soup boils. Force mixture through Foley Food Mill. Pour into blender container. Cover. Blend on highest speed until smooth, 30 to 45 seconds. Return to pan. Thin with cream to desired consistency. Stir in chicken. Reheat and serve. Excellent thinned with milk and served well chilled.

Hundreds of egg recipes can be prepared using the blender. I have selected a few well-known favorites and some new ones, the preparation of which is greatly aided by the blender. I am also including some cooking suggestions and information which my students have found helpful.

EGG DISHES

POACHED EGGS

Let us begin with instructions for poaching eggs since many people think they are tricky, time consuming and must be done at the last minute. Actually, poached eggs are none of the former and I encourage you to use them often. Let's tackle the last-minute bit first! Believe it or not, poached eggs can be kept successfully in a large bowl of tap water as hot as your hand can stand, if you keep replenishing the water as it cools. The easiest way to ensure perfectly shaped poached eggs is to be sure that the eggs you use are fresh since the older the egg, the less your chances of success. By following these simple instructions, I can guarantee you will serve nicely shaped poached eggs everytime.

To properly poach an egg, fill a large, lightly greased skillet ⅔ full with hot water. Add a little salt and 1 teaspoon of white vinegar. Bring to a full boil. Have the eggs ready—either at room temperature or warmed by running them briefly under the hot tap water. Place the UNOPENED eggs in the boiling water for 10 seconds. (An easy way to count seconds is "one-Mississippi, two-Mississippi, three-Mississippi, etc.). After 10 Mississippis, remove the eggs from the boiling water. Lower the heat until the water is barely simmering. Carefully break the eggs directly into the water. After the last egg has been broken, increase the heat until the water is once again barely simmering. Allow the eggs to poach for an additional 4 minutes. Gently lift eggs from the pan with a slotted spoon. Place them on absorbent paper to drain, or drop them into a bowl of hot water as described above. And, that's all there is to it!

Now, let's explore some poached egg dishes.

EGGS BENEDICT

SERVES 6

6 eggs
2 egg yolks
2 Tbsp. lemon juice
Salt, cayenne pepper, to taste

½ cup hot, melted butter
6 English muffin halves
6 thin slices ham or Canadian bacon
Truffles or black olives

Poach eggs and keep warm as directed on page 28 while making Hollandaise Sauce. Combine egg yolks, lemon juice, salt, and cayenne in blender container. Cover. Blend on low speed until mixture is turning freely in blades. Slowly pour in hot butter. Continue blending only until sauce thickens. Toast and butter muffin halves and sauté ham in dry skillet. Assemble dish by placing a slice of ham on top of each muffin. Drain and dry eggs carefully. Place on ham. Spoon sauce over all. Garnish with thin slices of truffle or black olives.

SOUFFLÉS

You can easily avoid the disappointment of a soufflé which fails to rise, or even worse, falls flat on its way to the table. Consistently successful soufflés are easy to accomplish once you understand what goes on in the process of making one.

It is air that causes the soufflé to rise. Think of the stiffly beaten egg whites as hundreds of tiny balloons. When the air inside these little balloons is heated in the oven it expands, the balloons blow up and the soufflé rises. Just as over inflated balloons will burst, the egg white balloons will burst if you leave the soufflé in the oven too long because heat creates over-expansion and the skins become brittle.

Most American cookbooks call for cooking soufflés too long. For a six cup soufflé dish and a 375° oven, 17 minutes is ample. A good soufflé makes its own sauce and it is the dry soufflés which are failures.

Soufflés fall into two categories. In the first type, which includes cheese, chocolate, vegetable, and meaty soufflés, the base is not brought to the boiling point. In the second group, which includes all fruit and liqueur soufflés, the base is brought to a full boil to thicken it before adding the egg yolks and flavorings. It is necessary to start with a thick base since the additon of fruit or liqueur thins it considerably. The stiffly beaten egg whites are always folded into the base, never the other way around. This will mean transferring the base to a large bowl before adding the whites, but the success of your soufflé may well depend upon your using that extra bowl.

ASPARAGUS SOUFFLÉ

SERVES 4 TO 6

6 cup, well-buttered soufflé dish
1 lb. asparagus (approximately)
3 Tbsp. butter
1 small onion, quartered
3 Tbsp. flour

¾ cup milk
Salt, cayenne pepper
4 egg yolks
6 egg whites
Parmesan cheese

Preheat oven to 375°F. Cook asparagus in boiling, salted water. Drain. Purée a few pieces at a time, using blender, until there is 1 cup purée in blender container. Add butter, onion, flour, and milk. Cover. Blend on high speed 30 seconds. Pour into saucepan. Season with salt and cayenne. Cook over moderate heat, stirring until mixture begins to thicken. Remove from heat. Stir briskly to stop further cooking. Beat in egg yolks, one at a time. Correct seasoning. Turn into large bowl. Fold in egg whites which have been beaten until stiff, but not dry. Pour batter into prepared dish. Sprinkle lightly with Parmesan. Bake in preheated oven 17 to 18 minutes. Serve immediately.

CHEDDAR CHEESE SOUFFLÉ

SERVES 4 TO 6

6 cup soufflé dish, well-buttered
2 Tbsp. butter
2 Tbsp. flour
¾ cup milk

4 oz. sharp Cheddar cheese
Salt, cayenne pepper
4 egg yolks
6 egg whites

Preheat oven to 375°F. Into blender container put butter, flour, milk, salt, cayenne, and cheese, which has been broken into pieces. Cover. Blend on highest speed 30 seconds. Pour mixture into saucepan. Stir over moderate heat until sauce just begins to thicken. Remove from heat. Beat in egg yolks, one at a time. Turn into large bowl. Fold in egg whites which have been beaten until stiff, but not dry. Pour into prepared dish. Bake in preheated oven 17 to 18 minutes. Serve immediately.

SPINACH SOUFFLÉ

SERVES 4 TO 6

6 cup soufflé dish, well-buttered
1 bunch spinach
3 Tbsp. butter
1 small onion, quartered
3 Tbsp. flour

¾ cup milk
Salt, cayenne pepper, to taste
Pinch nutmeg
4 egg yolks
7 egg whites

Preheat oven to 375°F. Wash spinach well. Remove stems. If left on, they are apt to wrap around the shaft of the blender, damaging the motor. Put spinach in pot with only the water clinging to it after washing. Cook just until wilted. Drain well. Rinse in cold water. Squeeze small handfuls tightly until spinach is free of water. Chop coarsely. Place in blender container. Add butter, onion, flour, milk, salt, cayenne, and nutmeg. Cover. Blend on highest speed 15 to 30 seconds. Pour mixture into saucepan. Stir over moderate heat until mixture begins to thicken. Remove from heat. Stir rapidly to prevent further cooking. Beat in egg yolks, one at a time. Turn batter into large bowl. Fold in egg whites which have been beaten until stiff, but not dry. Pour into prepared dish. Bake in preheated oven 17 to 18 minutes. Serve immediately.

We used to eat fish because it was inexpensive, or Friday, but today neither of these reasons is valid. I am surprised to find that many people do not like fish and I feel that this is simply because they have never tasted it properly prepared.

Fish and shellfish are delicate and should be handled with gentleness. They may be fried, baked, broiled, poached or sautéed, but always with care. The best way to cook a certain kind of fish depends on whether it is fat, or lean and dry. Fat fish such as salmon, halibut, rock cod, red snapper, and albacore are usually baked or broiled. Lean fish are most delicious when fried or poached and served with a delicate sauce. Sole, flounder, trout, and swordfish are among those classified as lean. Shellfish of all kinds are rich in flavor and are usually prepared so as not to obscure their character. Avoid heavy sauces, long cooking and high temperature for all fish.

FISH

POACHED SALMON WITH HOLLANDAISE

Fresh salmon filet
2 cups dry white wine
Water

Salt, peppercorns, bay leaf
Sauce Hollandaise, page 90

Select a piece of salmon suitable for the number of servings desired. Wrap it securely in cheesecloth. Place on rack in large pan or poacher. Add wine and enough water to cover the fish. Season with salt, peppercorns, and bay leaf. Cover the pan or poacher and bring slowly to boil. Reduce the heat and simmer slowly for 15 to 30 minutes depending on size of the filet or number of servings you are preparing. Lift rack from pan and allow fish to drain. Next prepare the Hollandaise Sauce. Remove cheesecloth from fish. Place the fish onto a serving platter. Spread sauce carefully over salmon. Garnish with freshly ground black pepper and serve with tiny boiled new potatoes.

FILET OF SOLE GRAND DUC
SERVES 4 TO 6

6 filets of sole
Juice of 1 lemon
¾ cup dry white wine
½ cup water

1 bay leaf
3 to 4 peppercorns
½ tsp. salt
1 lb. asparagus

Wash sole in lemon juice and water. Fold filets in half, skin side in. Arrange in lightly buttered baking dish. Combine wine, water, bay leaf, peppercorns, and salt. Pour over fish. Cover closely with waxed paper. Poach in 350°F oven 15 minutes. While fish is poaching, cook asparagus using the Paul Mayer Method, page 58. Cut asparagus into ½ inch pieces. Put butter, flour, salt, cayenne, and liquid from fish in blender container. Cover. Blend on high speed 15 to 30 seconds, or until completely smooth. Pour into small saucepan. Stir over moderate heat until sauce boils. Thin to desired consistency with cream. Stir in asparagus pieces. Place fish briefly on absorbent paper. Arrange on flameproof serving dish. Pour sauce over filets. Sprinkle with grated Parmesan. Dot with butter. Run under hot broiler until surface is nicely browned.

BAKED SALMON MOUSSE

3 Tbsp. butter
2 tsp. flour
Salt, cayenne
½ tsp. dry mustard
⅓ cup milk
1¾ lb. salmon

3 egg yolks
2 Tbsp. sherry
Nutmeg, anchovy paste
3 egg whites
1 cup (½ pt.) whipping cream
Sauce Hollandaise, page 90

Place butter, flour, salt, cayenne, dry mustard, and milk in blender container. Cover. Blend on low speed 15 to 30 seconds. Pour into small saucepan. Stir over moderate heat until sauce boils. Return to blender container. Skin and bone salmon. Add salmon, egg yolks, sherry, and seasonings to sauce. Cover. Blend on high speed 30 seconds or until mixture is puréed. Turn into large bowl. Beat egg whites and cream until stiff. Fold into salmon mixture. Adjust seasonings. Pour into well-buttered molds. Place in pan of hot water. Press a small piece of paper against the surface of each mold to prevent over browning. Bake in 375°F oven 25 to 30 minutes or until mousse is set and tests done when probed with a toothpick. Remove from oven. Allow to rest 3 minutes. Unmold. Serve with Hollandaise Sauce.

FILET OF SOLE DUGLERE

SERVES 8

8 filets of sole
3 ripe tomatoes
2 Tbsp. fresh parsley
¼ cup butter

Salt, cayenne pepper
½–1 cup cream
Freshly grated Parmesan cheese
Butter

Poach filets following directions given in Filet of Sole Grand Duc on page 39. While fish is poaching, peel and seed tomatoes. Cut into small shreds or julienne. Chop parsley. Place butter, flour, salt, and pepper in blender container. Strain poaching liquid and add. Cover. Blend on high speed 15 to 30 seconds or until mixture is smooth. Pour into small saucepan. Stir over medium heat until mixture boils and becomes quite thick. Thin to a nice consistency with cream. Be careful not to thin too much. Add tomatoes and parsley. Drain fish. Place on absorbent paper a few moments to remove excess liquid. Arrange on flameproof serving dish. Pour sauce over filets. Sprinkle with Parmesan. Dot liberally with small pieces of butter. Run under hot broiler until surface is nicely browned.

TRUITE NANO

SERVES 4 TO 6

4 to 6 large trout	½ cup whipping cream
¾ cup dry white wine	4 tsp. parsley
½ cup water	4 tsp. chives
1 bay leaf	¼ cup raw spinach leaves
3 – 4 peppercorns	2 Tbsp. Parmesan cheese, grated
Salt	1 lemon, sliced
4 egg yolks	Arugula leaves

Bone each trout. Lay in a lightly buttered baking dish. Combine wine, water, bay leaf, peppercorns, and salt in a small bowl and pour over trout. Cover with wax paper and poach in 350°F oven for 15 minutes. Remove trout to serving dish and set aside but keep warm. Strain poaching liquid. Measure ½ cup of liquid into small saucepan. Boil and reduce it rapidly until it measures 2 tablespoons. Place in blender container with remaining ingredients. Cover tightly and blend on medium speed 30 seconds or until spinach is well chopped. Turn into small saucepan. Stir over low heat until sauce thickens and coats spoon. Spread over trout and serve hot. Sprinkle with Parmesan cheese and serve with a garnish of lemon slices and arugula leaves.

CREVETTES AU BEURRE DES HERBES

SERVES 4 TO 6

A memorable meal at Les Fougeres, a superlative restaurant in Albany, New York, began with this delicious creation of Shrimp with Herb Butter.

1 lb. medium, raw shrimp
Juice of 1 lemon
6 Tbsp. melted butter
1 medium onion
3–4 anchovy filets

6 pitted black olives
Small garlic clove
1 tsp. parsley
1 tsp. tarragon
1 cup dry white wine

Remove shells, vein, and tails from shrimp. Wash in water with lemon juice added. Drain. Place remaining ingredients in blender container. Cover. Blend on medium speed until chopped. Pour into large skillet. Cook briskly until wine is nearly gone. Add shrimp. Continue cooking until wine is completely gone and shrimp have turned pink. Toss frequently. Serve at once in small individual ramekins as a first course or over rice as an entrée.

Because of its versatility, chicken has been the mainstay of the great cuisines of the world and a favorite of almost every country. Second only to its need to be the freshest you can buy, is the importance of chicken being thoroughly cooked. One of the best tests I know is to place it on a white plate and then pierce the thigh with the tines of a fork. The juice which comes forth should be clear. If tinged with pink, it is not done enough.

Many of the recipes in this book were collected during my travels in Europe where meat has always been expensive. In some of the world's most elegant recipes, the amount of meat used is relatively small. It is the sauce, or stuffing or other additions which make these dishes unusual and delicious. Great care is given to their preparation and a little meat is made to go a long way. Most frequently it is braised, after being browned in butter, with other ingredients chosen to bring out its best flavor. Even when steak or rare roast beef is served, it is almost always accompanied by a special sauce.

POULTRY & MEAT

SAUTÉ SAUCE

2 Tbsp. butter
3 Tbsp. flour
1 cup milk
½ cup whipping cream
Salt, cayenne pepper to taste
2 egg yolks
⅛ tsp. paprika

Place butter, flour, milk, cream, salt, and cayenne in blender container. Cover. Blend on high speed 15 to 30 seconds. Pour into saucepan. Stir over moderate heat until mixture boils. Return to blender. Add egg yolks. Cover. Blend on low speed 10 seconds, or until yolks thicken sauce. Add paprika. Stop blender. Taste for seasoning. Correct if necessary. Use sauce as directed.

POULET SAUTÉ NOT SO SEC

2½–3 lb. chicken
Salt, pepper
3–4 Tbsp. butter
2 finely chopped onions

½ cup dry white wine
½ lb. mushroom caps
1 tsp. each parsley, chives, tarragon
Sauté Sauce, on left

Cut chicken into serving pieces. Season with salt and pepper. Melt butter in large skillet. Add onion. Place chicken pieces on top of onions. Cook 5 minutes, turning pieces frequently. Put remaining ingredients in blender container. Cover. Blend on low speed 15 to 30 seconds, or until mushrooms are chopped. Pour mixture over chicken. Cover pan. Lower heat. Simmer gently 25 minutes. Turn pieces once halfway through cooking time. (Make sauce while chicken is cooking.) When chicken is tender, remove lid. Allow liquid to cook away until contents of skillet are merely buttery. Arrange on serving platter. Pour sauce into skillet. Stir to combine with pan juices. Pour over chicken. Garnish as desired and serve.

SOUR CREAM SAUCE

2 tsp. Bovril
2 tsp. tomato paste
¼ cup flour
1 cup water

Measure Bovril, tomato paste, flour, and water in blender container. Cover. Run machine on high speed 15 seconds or until well mixed.

SWEDISH MEATBALLS IN SOUR CREAM SAUCE

SERVES 6

¾ lb. ground round
¾ lb. ground lean veal
2 cups bread cubes
Milk
1 medium onion, quartered
¼ cup melted butter
3 eggs
Salt & pepper, to taste

2 tsp. nutmeg
2 tsp. paprika
1 tsp. dry mustard
1 tsp. dried dill weed
3 Tbsp. butter
1 clove garlic, minced
2 cups (1 pt.) sour cream (room temperature)
1 Tbsp. dried dill weed

Place meat in large mixing bowl. Soak bread cubes in a small amount of milk. Squeeze bread almost dry. Crumble into bowl with meat. Put onion pieces and melted butter into blender container. Cover. Run blender on low speed about 20 seconds, or until onion is chopped. Turn into small skillet. Sauté until onion begins to brown. Add to meat. Break eggs into blender container. Add salt, pepper, nutmeg, paprika, dry mustard, and dill weed. Cover. Run blender on highest speed 15 to 30 seconds, or until thoroughly blended. Add to meat. Work mixture together with hands. Shape meat into small balls.

Melt butter in large skillet. Brown meatballs quickly, but thoroughly. Remove from pan. Add garlic to drippings. Cook slowly, 2 minutes. Add Sour Cream Sauce (recipe on left) to garlic. Stir over medium heat until sauce thickens and boils. Remove from heat. Carefully stir in sour cream and dill weed. Add meatballs to sauce. Simmer gently 5 to 7 minutes before serving.

SUPREMA POLLO FARCITA

SERVES 6

6 chicken breast halves
3 small zucchini
¼ lb. Fontina cheese
¼ lb. Parmesan cheese

¼ cup butter
2 Tbsp. olive oil
3 Tbsp. Marsala wine
2 Tbsp. cream

Bone breasts. Place between two sheets of waxed paper. Pound gently until very thin. (Avoid tearing the flesh.) Cut zucchini and cheese into chunks. Put into blender container. Cover. Blend on low speed 15 to 30 seconds or until zucchini is chopped and mixed with cheese. Place a spoonful of this mixture in the center of each piece of breast. Fold breast over filling, making tightly closed packages. Tie each with string. Dust lightly with flour. Melt butter in skillet. Cook breasts slowly in hot butter about 15 to 20 minutes. Turn frequently so cheese will melt and zucchini will be cooked. When done, remove to a serving dish. Add olive oil, Marsala, and cream to the skillet. Cook until sauce thickens. Pour sauce over chicken. Run under the broiler to brown the sauce.

BARBECUED SPARERIBS

3 lb. meaty spareribs
1 Tbsp. butter or bacon fat
½ small onion
½ cup water
2 Tbsp. tarragon vinegar
1 Tbsp. Worcestershire sauce

¼ cup lemon juice
1 Tbsp. light brown sugar
1 bottle (12 oz.) chili sauce
½ tsp. salt
¼ tsp. paprika

Cut spareribs into serving-sized pieces. When ready to prepare, put remaining ingredients in blender container. Cover. Blend on low speed 15 to 30 seconds, or until onion is chopped and blended with other ingredients. Pour mixture into a large skillet. Simmer over low heat 20 minutes. While sauce is simmering, place ribs in a large baking pan. Cover with foil. Bake in 500°F oven 15 minutes. Lower heat to 350°F. Pour sauce over ribs. Continue baking about one hour, or until sauce dries out somewhat and meat is soft to the point of leaving the bones. Baste every 10 minutes, or so, with pan drippings. Turn pieces once during baking.

VEAL CORDON BLEU

SERVES 6

6 slices veal
6 slices boiled ham
6 slices Gruyère cheese
1 egg

1 tsp. water
Flour
Fine dry bread crumbs
Hot deep fat (380°F)

Trim veal. Place between pieces of waxed paper. Pound with a mallet until very thin. Beat egg and water together. Remove top sheet of waxed paper. Paint each veal slice with egg. Place ham on one half of each veal slice. Lay cheese on top of ham. Fold veal over cheese to make a sealed package. Dip in flour, then beaten egg, then crumbs. Fry in hot fat until deeply browned and crisp. Drain on absorbent paper and serve.

PAUL'S MEAT LOAF

1½ lb. ground chuck or round steak
4 slices firm white bread
Milk
Salt, black pepper

1 small onion, cut into pieces
3 Tbsp. chili sauce
3–5 Tbsp. mayonnaise

Crumble meat into mixing bowl. Soak bread in milk. Squeeze dry. Put into blender container. Add remaining ingredients. Cover. Blend on low speed 15 to 30 seconds or until everything is chopped and well mixed. Add to meat. Mix thoroughly with hands. Correct seasoning. Pack into well-greased loaf pan. Spread entire surface with more chili sauce. Bake in 350°F oven 30 to 45 minutes. Do not overcook or meat loaf will become dry. Remove from oven. Allow to rest at least 5 minutes before removing from pan. Slice. Serve as is, or with a tomato sauce of your choice. Cool, then wrap in foil if it is to be served cold. Chill for easier slicing.

POULET EN CRÈME SAUCE

SERVES 6

3½ lb. chicken
2 onions
2 carrots
2 stalks celery
Salt, peppercorns
1 bay leaf

¼ cup butter
¼ cup flour
1 cup milk
1 cup (½ pt.) whipping cream
4 egg yolks
¼ tsp. paprika

Place trussed chicken in Dutch oven or deep kettle. Coarsely chop onions, carrots, and celery. Add to pot along with salt, peppercorns, and bay leaf. Barely cover chicken with water. Bring slowly to boil. Reduce heat. Simmer gently 30 minutes or until chicken is thoroughly cooked, but not overly so. (One of the best tests I know for testing chicken is to pierce the thigh with the tines of a fork. The juice should run clear. If it is tinged with pink the chicken is not done). Remove chicken from pot. When cool enough to handle remove meat from chicken. Cut in fairly large cubes. Turn up the heat under the kettle. Quickly reduce broth until it measures 1 cup. Strain out vegetables. Pour reduced broth into blender container with butter, flour, milk, whipping cream, salt, and cayenne. Cover. Blend on high speed from 15 to 30 seconds, or until everything is well mixed. Pour into saucepan. Stir over moderate heat until mixture boils. Return to blender. Add egg yolks. Cover. Blend on low speed 15 seconds or until yolks have thickened the sauce. Add paprika. Blend 5 seconds. Add diced chicken to sauce. Heat gently to serving temperature. Do not allow to boil, lest it curdle.

Fresh vegetables, carefully prepared, are one of the true pleasures of the table. Not only do they add flavor and texture to a meal, but beautiful color as well. It is extremely important to cook vegetables in such a way as to preserve their bright color and firm texture. Nothing destroys vegetables so completely as overcooking. My special method for cooking fresh green vegetables is given on the next page.

The recipes which I have chosen to present here are a little different, and dressed up a bit, since my students are always requesting new ways of preparing vegetables, especially for entertaining. These particular dishes are designed to be served with simply prepared entrées, such as roasts, chops, or steaks. When serving richly sauced entrées, be sure to keep the vegetables as simple and unassuming as possible. In almost every case, these recipes can be prepared in advance with only a few minutes cooking time needed just before serving.

VEGETABLES

PAUL'S METHOD FOR COOKING GREEN VEGETABLES

First off, let us consider a way of cooking green vegetables which is guaranteed to retain their color, texture and flavor. This method, if followed exactly, will yield brilliant, delicious peas, green beans, brussels sprouts, asparagus, and broccoli. It does not apply to root vegetables, eggplant, artichokes, or spinach. Don't ask me why it works, but it works! I think it's because boiling water is poured into a hot pan so it boils immediately and never stops during the entire cooking process. If vegetables are dropped into boiling water, or if boiling water is poured over them, the water stops boiling immediately. It takes a while for it to return to a full boil, during which time the vegetables just soak instead of cooking.

Have a tea kettle full of rapidly boiling water. In another pot, with a lid, put a large handful of sugar and 1 teaspoon salt. Place over high heat until sugar just begins to caramelize. Place prepared vegetables in pot, and with the heat still at the highest point, pour in the boiling water. Clap on the lid and boil furiously for 7 minutes—not 8, or 6, or 5½, or 9—but 7 minutes. Quickly drain the vegetables. Rinse briefly with cold water to stop the cooking. (The vegetable will stay hot!) Drain and season with salt, pepper, and a little melted butter.

ASPERGES NEAPOLITAINE

1 lb. asparagus spears
3 Tbsp. butter
2 celery stalks
1 small onion
Small piece of Parmesan cheese

1 Tbsp. fresh bread
1 can (8 oz.) Italian-style tomatoes
Salt, freshly ground pepper
Pinch sugar, thyme, oregano

Wash asparagus tips well. Dry thoroughly. Melt butter in an ovenproof dish. Lay asparagus in even rows in dish. Trim celery and peel with potato peeler to remove strings. Place celery, onion, Parmesan, bread, well-drained tomatoes (no juice) and seasonings in blender container. Cover. Blend on high speed 15 seconds or until cheese is grated. Spread mixture over asparagus. Bake in 375°F oven 35 to 40 minutes.

FAGIOLINI ET POMADORO
(STRING BEANS & TOMATOES)

SERVES 6

4 ripe tomatoes
3 Tbsp. olive oil
1 large onion, cut in chunks

1 large garlic clove
1 tsp. crushed basil
2 lb. green beans, trimmed

Remove skins from tomatoes by holding them in boiling water 10 seconds. Place under cold running water immediately to stop further cooking. Cut away hard centers and remove seeds. Put tomatoes, olive oil, onion chunks, garlic, sugar, and basil in blender container. Cover. Blend on high speed only long enough to chop vegetables, about 15 seconds. Pour into large skillet. Reduce juices rapidly over medium high heat until mixture is fairly thick. Cook beans using the Paul Mayer Method, page 58. Drain thoroughly. Combine with tomato mixture. Reheat only as long as necessary. Overcooking will destroy the bright green color of the beans.

SPINACH BARNET

SERVES 6

3 bunches fresh spinach
3 Tbsp. butter
2 onions
¼ cup flour

1 tsp. Bovril
¾ cup strong beef broth
Salt, pepper

Wash spinach well. Boil spinach just until tender and remove from water quickly. Squeeze it as dry as possible with hands. Remove heavy stems and chop coarsely. Place in blender container with remaining ingredients and cover tightly. Blend on medium speed about 1 minute or until onion and spinach are chopped and ingredients are mixed. Turn mixture into heavy skillet. Stir over moderate heat until mixture thickens and boils, and is the consistency of heavy creamed spinach. Serve as is with hot toast or crackers or use in the recipe that follows.

MUSHROOMS STUFFED WITH SPINACH

SERVES 12

24 giant mushrooms
Butter
Spinach Barnet, page 62

Swiss cheese
Parmesan cheese

Remove stems from mushrooms. Save for another use. Clean mushrooms by brushing with a damp paper towel. Sauté quickly in very hot butter. Do not overcook. Place mushrooms in baking dish, stem side up. Fill hollows with Spinach Barnet. Grate Swiss cheese in blender. Combine with Parmesan. Sprinkle over filled mushrooms. Bake in 425°F oven until cheese melts and tops are browned and crusty.

EGGPLANT DU PAYS PROVENÇALE

SERVES 6

2 medium-sized eggplants
Butter
2 lb. tomatoes
3 Tbsp. olive oil
2 cloves garlic
1 stalk celery, chopped

1 Tbsp. parsley
1 coarsely chopped carrot
1 onion, cut into chunks
Salt, pepper, basil
Gruyère cheese

Wash and dry eggplants. Do not peel. Cut into strips 4 to 5 inches long, 2 inches wide and about ½ inch thick. Dredge in flour. Shake off excess flour. Fry strips gently in foaming butter, until nicely browned. Peel, seed, and quarter tomatoes. Place in blender container with olive oil, garlic, celery, parsley, carrot, and onion. Cover. Blend 20 seconds. Season highly. Pour into large skillet. Cook over medium heat until sauce reduces to a nicely thickened consistency. Remove from heat. Place a layer of eggplant strips in the bottom of a shallow baking dish. Spread some of sauce over strips. Top with a layer of grated Gruyère. Repeat in same order until dish is filled. End with cheese on top. Bake in 400°F oven 20 to 30 minutes, or until dish is sizzling and cheese is melted and golden brown. Allow to rest 5 minutes, to re-absorb oil, before serving.

CELERIAC AU GRATIN

SERVES 6

3 lb. celery root
6 Tbsp. butter
6 Tbsp. flour
Salt, cayenne pepper

1 cup (½ pt.) whipping cream
½ cup grated Parmesan cheese
Pinch dry mustard
Fresh, buttered bread crumbs

Peel and dice celery root. Keep in water, with a little lemon juice or vinegar added, until ready to cook. Drain. Barely cover with fresh water. Add a little salt. Bring slowly to boil. Cook until barely tender, about 10 minutes. Drain well. Strain liquid. Reserve 1½ cups. Place butter, flour, salt, cayenne, cream, and reserved liquid in blender container. Cover. Blend on high speed 20 seconds. Pour into saucepan. Stir over moderate heat until mixture thickens and boils. Add Parmesan and mustard. Allow to boil, stirring constantly, 2 minutes. Remove from heat. Add celery root. Mix well. Pour into large, flat casserole. Cover with a heavy layer of buttered bread crumbs. Dust with Parmesan. Bake in 350°F oven 30 minutes, or until crumbs are browned and sauce bubbly.

QUICHE DE POIS

SERVES 4 TO 6

½ cup (¼ lb.) firm butter
2 oz. Ricotta cheese
¾ cup flour
1 pkg. (10 oz.) frozen peas

1 cup (½ pt.) whipping cream
4 eggs yolks
Salt, cayenne, nutmeg

Blend butter, cheese, and flour together. Form into ball. Roll out on pastry cloth. Fit pastry into 8-inch layer cake pan. Rinse peas under running hot water until loosened from block. Drain on paper towels. Fill pastry with peas. Place cream, egg yolks and seasonings in blender container. Cover. Blend on highest speed 15 seconds or until yolks are well mixed with cream. Pour mixture over peas. Bake in 375°F oven 45 to 50 minutes or until top is deeply browned and custard tests done when knife inserted in center comes out clean. Remove from oven. Allow to stand 2 minutes. Invert pan onto a plate. Remove pan. Reinvert onto another plate immediately to have tart free standing and upright.

MUSHROOMS WITH GARLIC & HERBS

SERVES 6

½ cup (¼ lb.) butter
4 finely minced shallots
1½ lb. small, whole mushrooms
Salt and pepper
4 oz. Cognac
3 peeled garlic cloves

1 Tbsp. parsley
½ tsp. each turmeric, cumin, coriander,
   ginger, pepper
1 tsp. each rosemary, thyme, basil
3 cups whipping cream
Butter

Melt butter in skillet. Add shallots and mushrooms. Sauté 2 minutes. Season. Pour in Cognac. Ignite. Put garlic, parsley, turmeric, cumin, coriander, ginger, and pepper in blender container. Cover. Blend on highest speed until thoroughly minced and mixed. Add rosemary, thyme, basil, and whipping cream. Cover. Blend until pulverized and mixed. Pour mixture over mushrooms. Continue cooking fairly rapidly until sauce begins to thicken. Add extra butter, one tablespoon at a time, until mixture thickens further, and does not follow the spoon when stirred across the bottom of the pan. Serve in individual ramekins. Sprinkle with finely chopped parsley.

Think of green salad as a hyphen. It connects the entrée with the dessert and was designed as a palate cleanser. It was never meant to be served at the beginning of a meal! There are so many atrocities committed in the name of "salad" that when one finally does have a great one, it's like finding a pearl in an oyster. The best I ever ate was served at a French inn called Auberge des Ternpliers, about 75 miles from Paris. It was so delicious I had to know the secret. Mild, yet piquant, it was obiviously not made with olive oil. Presistent questioning elicited the fact that the oil was "huile de berry." It was only out of complete exasperation at my prying that the maitre d'hotel finally brought out a "berry," and I discovered it was nothing more than a walnut! The delicious salad was made with walnut oil and the blandest of white wine vinegar. Walnut oil is available in health food stores and I heartily recommend it.

SALADS

JUST RIGHT FRENCH DRESSING

So-called "French" dressing can be made most successfully in the blender, but I hesitate to give you anything like a definite recipe for it, since its preparation depends so very much upon individual tastes. However, I can suggest a method by which you can arrive at just the right proportion of oil to vinegar to please you.

Start with equal amounts of oil and vinegar in the blender container. Season to your liking with salt, paprika, and dry mustard. Cover container. Blend on low speed about 5 seconds. Taste the result. It will be far too tart! Start adding oil 2 tablespoons at a time. Blend. Taste. Continue in this fashion until you have a combination that pleases you. Measure the amount of dressing you have. If you started with ½ cup of oil and ½ cup of vinegar, and after adding and tasting, the final amount measures 1½ cups you will have added another ½ cup of oil. The ratio of oil to vinegar that pleases you is 2 to 1. Make a note of this ratio. Always make your dressings to that measurement and it will be perfect every time.

TOMATO-AVOCADO-EGG-RED ONION SALAD

SERVES 6 TO 8

Another Paul Mayer original.

3 small tomatoes
3 hard cooked eggs
1 avocado, sliced
3 small red onions, thinly sliced
1½ cups olive oil

½ cup tarragon vinegar
Salt, black pepper
Pinch dry mustard, paprika
¼ tsp. marjoram
3 heads butter lettuce

Peel tomatoes and eggs. Cut each into eighths. Place in large mixing bowl with avocado and onion slices. Combine oil, vinegar, salt, pepper, mustard, paprika, and marjoram in blender container. Cover. Blend on low speed 5 seconds. Pour over ingredients in bowl. Allow to marinate as long as possible. Wash and dry lettuce leaves well. Tear large ones if necessary. Arrange in salad bowl. Add marinated ingredients and dressing. Toss lightly until each leaf is coated with dressing. Serve.

ASPERGES VINAIGRETTE

SERVES 6 TO 8

2 lb. asparagus
2 to 3 Tbsp. Kosher-style dill pickle pieces
1 cup olive oil
½ cup tarragon vinegar

Salt, pepper
Pinch dry mustard, paprika
2 to 3 Tbsp. each capers, chives

Cook asparagus according to the Paul Mayer Method on page 58. Drain and dry. Chill. Remove seeds from pickles. Combine with remaining ingredients in blender container. Cover. Blend on low speed 5 seconds only. To serve, arrange chilled asparagus on salad plates. Spoon dressing over asparagus. Serve well chilled.

SALAD DE POMMES DE TERRE

SERVES 4 TO 6

2 lb. tiny new potatoes
Salt, pepper
⅓ cup hot bouillon
1 tiny onion
1 Tbsp. white wine vinegar

3 Tbsp. olive oil
⅛ tsp. dry mustard
¼ tsp. water
1½ Tbsp. chopped parsley
½ tsp. each dried chervil, basil, tarragon

Peel and slice potatoes ½-inch thick. Cook in boiling salted water just until tender, 5 to 10 minutes. Do not overcook. Drain thoroughly. Place hot slices in mixing bowl. Season with salt and pepper. Add hot bouillon. Toss carefully until all liquid is absorbed. Place remaining ingredients in blender container. Cover. Blend on low speed 5 seconds. Pour over potato slices. Toss carefully. Serve at room temperature.

CHICKEN SALAD

SERVES 6

6 Tbsp. butter
6 chicken breast halves
2 cups milk
6 hard-cooked eggs
½ cup celery

6 Tbsp. olive oil
3 Tbsp. tarragon vinegar
Salt, pepper, paprika
Sauce Mayonnaise, page 93

Stuff 1 tablespoon butter under the skin of each breast. Lay breasts skin side up in a roasting pan. Add milk. Bake in 375°F oven 30 minutes or until skin puffs and turns crispy brown. Baste frequently with milk. Remove breasts from pan. Chill. When breasts are chilled, remove skin. Cut meat into medium-sized chunks. Slice eggs. Chop celery as fine as you possibly can. Carefully mix chicken, egg slices, and celery together in large bowl. Combine olive oil, vinegar, salt, pepper, and paprika in blender container. Cover. Blend on high speed until well mixed. Pour over chicken mixture. Allow to marinate several hours or overnight if possible. Make Sauce Mayonnaise as directed. Add enough to chicken to bind. Chill the salad thoroughly. Turn out on a bed of lettuce. Frost with a thin layer of Sauce Mayonnaise. Garnish with more sliced eggs and capers, if desired.

Although the following dessert recipes are all made easier through the use of the blender, they are as varied as one could imagine. There are light, elegant ones, old-fashioned steamed puddings and some unusual ones. All of them are delicious.

I have included the crepe, that universally enjoyed queen of the pancake dishes. A blender is its perfect companion. I have collected recipes for crepes from many restaurants throughout Europe and a couple outstanding dessert ones are included here.

All of the desserts are delightful treats which will add the proper finishing touch to your dinner menus. Most are served in small portions to accompany a demitasse of your favorite coffee.

DESSERTS

CHOCOLATE SOUFFLÉ

Chocolate soufflés do not, as a rule, rise quite as high as other kinds. One-third the depth out of the dish is considered a success.

6 cup soufflé dish, well-buttered
2 oz. bitter chocolate
¾ cup milk
3 Tbsp. butter

3 Tbsp. flour
½ cup sugar
5 egg yolks
7 egg whites

Preheat oven to 375°F. Sprinkle buttered dish with a little sugar. Melt chocolate in milk over low heat. Pour into blender container. Add butter, flour, and 6 tablespoons sugar. Blend on high speed until everything is well blended. Pour into saucepan. Stir over moderate heat until sauce just begins to thicken. Remove from heat. Rapidly beat in egg yolks all at once. Transfer mixture to large bowl. Beat egg whites until stiff. Add remaining sugar. Continue beating 30 seconds. Fold into base. Pour into prepared dish. Bake in preheated oven 18 minutes. Serve at once.

VANILLA RUM SAUCE

6 egg yolks
1 cup half and half
1 cup whipping cream
1 teaspoon vanilla
¼ cup rum
½ cup sugar

Measure all ingredients into blender container. Cover. Blend on high speed 10 to 15 seconds or until well mixed. Pour into top of double boiler. Cook over, but not touching, boiling water. Stir constantly until mixture thickens. Remove from hot water. Set pan in ice water until warm. Keep warm for serving.

STEAMED CHOCOLATE PUDDING

2 oz. bitter chocolate
1 egg
½ cup sugar
1 Tbsp. butter
1 Tbsp. red current jelly

1 cup flour
1 tsp. baking powder
⅛ tsp. salt
½ cup milk
Vanilla Rum Sauce, on left

Melt chocolate over lowest heat or hot, not boiling, water. Pour into blender with remaining ingredients. Cover. Blend on low speed 30 seconds to one minute or until ingredients are well mixed. Pour batter into well-greased pudding mold. If you are an optimist, grease the inside of the lid as well. Seal the mold tightly. Stand on a rack in a large kettle. Add as much boiling water as possible without having mold float. Steam for one hour. Add boiling water as necessary to keep level of water up. Unmold on a platter. Serve with Vanilla Rum Sauce.

LIQUEUR SOUFFLÉ

8 cup soufflé dish, well-buttered
3 Tbsp. butter
3 Tbsp. flour
¾ cup milk

5 egg yolks
2 Tbsp. plus 2 tsp. sugar
6 Tbsp. liqueur*
7 egg whites

Preheat oven to 375°F. Sprinkle dish with a little sugar. Tie a collar of buttered waxed paper around rim of dish. Place butter, flour, and milk in blender container. Cover. Blend on high speed 15 to 30 seconds. Pour into small saucepan. Stir over moderate heat until mixture thickens and boils. Remove from heat. Combine egg yolks with 2 tablespoons sugar. Rapidly beat into sauce. Add liqueur. Transfer to a large bowl. Beat egg whites until stiff but not cry. Add 2 teaspoons sugar. Beat 30 seconds. Fold into liqueur base. Pour into prepared dish. Bake in preheated oven 20 to 22 minutes.

Use any liqueur or combination of liqueurs you wish. Some good combinations are crème de banana and white crème de menthe; apricot and raspberry; white crème de cacao and Cherry Heering; white crème de cacao and Grand Marnier.

CREPES

Undeniably the queen of the frying pan cake is the crepe. Almost every recipe for crepes which I have seen has stipulated that the batter must rest at least 30 minutes before beginning to make the pancakes. Not so when made with a blender, I have discovered! The pancakes produced in the following fashion come out light, well-textured, and tender. They may be made well in advance of the time at which they are to be finished, and stored one on top of the other, with nothing in between them. The best way is on a wooden board with a large bowl inverted over them. Similarly stacked they may be wrapped in aluminum foil and frozen. The only word of caution here is to be sure that you allow them to thaw completely before trying to separate them.

Now! Just a word or two about making the crepes! How easy that sounds! And easy it really is, if you observe one or two rules. First and foremost! Reserve a pan exclusively for making them! DO NOT WASH IT EVER! A teflon pan will do admirably, but it, too, should never be washed, merely wiped clean with paper toweling after each use. If you are using a metal pan, one made of cast iron or cast aluminum is best, and it should be treated before its first use in the following manner: Spread the surface of the pan with vegetable oil, and allow the pan to rest in this fashion for 24 hours. Then, with the oil still in the pan, heat it until it smokes. Turn off the heat and with the oil remaining in the pan allow the pan to cool until it is completely cold. Then, pour off the oil, and wipe the pan dry with paper toweling. Your pan should then be ready for the first crepe. If it should stick at this point, retreat it as above, try again until you make a crepe that will not stick. After that, provided some well-meaning soul doesn't do you a favor and wash your pan, you should have no further troubles. Just follow the basic recipe and directions following on page 83.

BLENDER CREPES

When making dessert crepes, increase sugar to 3 tablespoons.

1½ cups milk	3 Tbsp. butter, cooled
3 eggs	3 Tbsp. brandy
Grated rind of ½ lemon	⅞ cup flour*
1 tsp. sugar	

Measure ingredients into blender container in the order listed. Cover. Blend on medium speed only as long as necessary to mix everything well, about 15 to 30 seconds. Pour batter into bowl. Cook crepes in the following manner:

Butter a 5 or 6 inch skillet lightly, for the first crepe only. Tip pan and slowly pour in crepe batter, just coating bottom of pan, about 2 tablespoons. Tilt the pan immediately so that the batter will completely spread over the entire bottom of the pan. Cook quickly on moderate heat until edges begin to brown. Loosen around edges with a thin spatula. Grasp crepe firmly with both hands and flip it over. Cook on reverse side 5 seconds only. Turn crepe out onto plate. Continue cooking crepes without adding butter to pan, until all batter is used.

Measure 1 cup, remove 2 tablespoons.

If you are especially adept it is possible to use two crepe pans at once, filling one and then the other, and finally turning them out in the same order, leaving you two empty crepe pans with which to begin again.

Using a small crepe pan and a minimum amount of batter for each crepe, the basic recipe should yield 18 to 24 crepes. Once you have mastered the process of making the little fellows, make them often. Serve with super fillings and sauce and delight your guests and family with crepes, crepes, and more crepes. The crepes themselves freeze perfectly. Make them ahead and keep on hand at all times. Leftovers wrapped in a crepe and served with a delicious sauce, become a beautifully disguised entrée.

CREPES SUZETTE

SERVES 6

Blender Crepes, page 83
12 lumps sugar
2 oranges

⅓ cup sweet butter
3 oz. Grand Marnier
4 oz. fine brandy

Prepare crepes according to directions. Rub sugar lumps over orange skins to absorb zest. Then squeeze juice from oranges. Melt butter in the blazing pan of a chafing dish. Add orange juice and sugar lumps. Heat until mixture is bubbling and sugar has dissolved. Add Grand Marnier. Ignite. Spoon the liquid up to aerate the liqueur. Continue until flame goes out. Bathe each crepe in sauce before folding into quarters. Pull crepes to one side of pan. Add brandy, and ignite. Baste crepes with flaming sauce and if possible serve while still blazing. Allow 3 crepes for each serving.

CREPES MEXICAINE

SERVES 6 TO 8

I was served this bit of ambrosia at the Hotel Prinses Juliana in Valeknburg, Netherlands. The weather was horrible but the food was out of this world!

Blender Crepes, page 83
2½ Tbsp. fine sugar
½ cup strong, fresh coffee
1 tsp. instant coffee
3 – 4 drops lemon juice

2 oz. Kahlua
2 oz. Kirsch
Coffee flavored ice cream
Whipped cream
Sliced toasted almonds

Make crepes as directed. Fold into quarters. Melt sugar in the blazing pan of a chafing dish. Add coffee slowly so it boils without stopping. Add instant coffee and lemon juice. Place folded crepes in blazing pan. Pour Kahlua over them. Ignite. When flame goes out add Kirsch. Ignite again. Remove crepes from pan. Open and fill each one with softened ice cream. Close again over ice cream. Place on dessert plates. Spoon sauce over each one. Garnish with whipped cream and almonds.

The blender is a great time saver in sauce making. Difficult-to-make egg-based sauces become easy and almost foolproof. And, when making cream sauces, all ingredients are blended together a few seconds then poured into a saucepan and quickly cooked as directed. Because of the complete success of these methods, I probably use my blender more for saucemaking than for any other one purpose.

There are literally thousands of sauces, all of which stem from a basic few—much in the manner of a family tree. The great French chefs would undoubtedly be horrified at the thought of taking shortcuts with their creations, yet this is precisely what we shall do with these blender sauce recipes which are true gourmet delights. I have gathered together my favorites and those which I think you will use most often. After you have tried them, I hope you will use the blender to make your own favorites this easy, new way.

SAUCES

SAUCE BECHAMEL

MAKES 1 CUP

2 Tbsp. butter
2 Tbsp. flour
2½ cups milk
Pinch powdered thyme

Pinch nutmeg
Salt, cayenne pepper
Small bay leaf

Place butter, flour, milk, thyme, nutmeg, salt, and cayenne in blender container. Cover. Blend on high speed 15 to 30 seconds. Pour into saucepan. Cook over moderate heat, stirring constantly, until mixture comes to a boil. Add bay leaf. Lower heat. Simmer 45 minutes or until sauce is thickened and reduced to 1 cup. Strain. Use as is or as directed in other recipes.

SAUCE NANTUA

This subtle delicate sauce is delicious over poached fish, eggs, and salmon.

1 cup Sauce Bechamel, page 88
½ lb. medium-sized shrimp
White wine
Salt

½ cup (¼ lb.) butter, melted
¼ cup whipping cream
1 Tbsp. brandy
Dash cayenne pepper

Reduce Sauce Bechamel over low heat until it measures ½ cup. Cover with plastic wrap pressed tightly against surface of the sauce. Set aside. Cook shrimp by first barely covering them with equal amounts of water and wine. Add a little salt. Bring to full boil. Remove shrimp from pan. Cool quickly under cold running water. Boil cooking liquid down to 2 tablespoons. Blend into the thickened Bechamel. Shell shrimp. Put shells into blender container with melted butter. Run on low speed 30 to 60 seconds, or until shells are pulverized. Strain through fine sieve or cheesecloth. Add 6 tablespoons of the shrimp butter, whipping cream, brandy, and cayenne to sauce. Mix thoroughly.

SAUCE HOLLANDAISE
MAKES ABOUT 1 CUP

2 egg yolks
1 to 2 Tbsp. lemon juice

Salt, cayenne pepper, to taste
½ cup (¼ lb.) butter, melted

Place egg yolks, lemon juice, salt, and cayenne in blender. Cover. Blend on low speed 5 seconds. Remove cap. Pour in butter, in a slow steady stream. Continue blending only until sauce has thickened. (Should it curdle, add 2 additional egg yolks. Blend at high speed while adding whipping cream 1 tablespoon at a time until sauce reconstitutes.)

SAUCE BEARNAISE

MAKES ABOUT ¾ CUP

For grilled meats, serve Hollandaise's first cousin.

4 shallots
½ cup tarragon vinegar
2 egg yolks
Salt

Cayenne pepper
1 tsp. each parsley, chives, tarragon
½ cup (¼ lb.) melted butter, cooled

Place shallots and vinegar in blender container. Cover. Run blender on low speed 10 to 15 seconds or until shallots are chopped. Pour mixture into small saucepan. Reduce until it measures 2 tablespoons. Strain out shallots. Pour strained vinegar back into blender container. Add egg yolks, salt, cayenne, parsley, chives, and tarragon. Cover. Blend on lowest speed. Remove cap, not cover. Gradually pour in cooled butter. As soon as sauce thickens, stop blending.

SAUCE MORNAY

A bed of cooked spinach, poached eggs, and golden Sauce Mornay, run under the broiler to glaze and brown the sauce, and you have Poached Eggs Florentine. The star of the production is this really grand and rich sauce.

2 Tbsp. butter	½ cup Gruyère cheese
2 Tbsp. flour	2 Tbsp. Parmesan cheese
1 cup cream	Dry mustard
Salt, cayenne pepper	2 egg yolks

Measure butter, flour, cream, salt, and cayenne into blender container. Cover. Blend on high speed for 15 to 30 seconds. Add Gruyère and Parmesan. Blend 15 seconds. Pour into saucepan. Cook, stirring, until mixture comes to boil. Add a pinch of dry mustard. (Do not worry if sauce separates at this point.) Return to blender container. Add egg yolks. Cover. Blend on high speed until smooth and shiny. Keep warm over hot, but not boiling, water. Press plastic wrap down against surface to exclude all air and prevent top from drying. Makes 1½ cups.

SAUCE MAYONNAISE

MAKES 1 QUART

3 whole eggs
2¼ tsp. salt
1½ tsp. dry mustard
Pinch paprika

6 Tbsp. white vinegar or 6 Tbsp.
   lemon juice or 3 Tbsp. of each
3½ cups oil

Place eggs, salt, mustard, paprika, vinegar (or lemon juice), and
¾ cup oil in blender container. Cover. Blend on highest speed 5
seconds or until mixed. Remove cap from cover. Start adding oil
in a slow but steady stream. Pour directly into the center of the
whirlpool formed by the swirling mixture. Pour steadily until the
whirlpool disappears completely. This should use 1½ to 2 cups of
the oil. Continue adding oil, a little at a time. The mayonnaise will
become thicker and thicker. Add the oil in this manner until it is all
gone. Never add more oil until each addition is completely worked
in. Keep blender on highest speed all the time.

SAUCE MAYONNAISE RAVIGOTE
MAKES ABOUT 1½ CUPS

For a change try this one with beautifully crisp fried fish instead of tartar sauce—you'll never go back.

2 Tbsp. each capers, chervil, parsley, shallots, and onion
¼ cup dry white wine
1 Tbsp. strained lemon juice

½ tsp. anchovy paste
1 hard-cooked egg white, finely chopped
1 cup Sauce Mayonnaise (page 93)

Measure capers, chervil, parsley, shallots, onion, wine, and lemon juice into blender container. Blend on low speed about 10 seconds. Pour mixture into saucepan. Cook very gently 15 minutes. Pour into a large bowl. Cool. Add anchovy paste and egg white. Beat in mayonnaise. Chill thoroughly before serving.

INDEX